125 YEARS AT MISSISSIPPI STATE UNIVERSITY

A PICTORIAL HISTORY OF THE PEOPLE'S UNIVERSITY

125 YEARS AT
MISSISSIPPI
STATE
UNIVERSITY

A PICTORIAL HISTORY OF

THE PEOPLE'S UNIVERSITY

Mississippi State
UNIVERSITY
125 YEARS
1878—2003

Library of Congress Catalog Card Number 2003108738

ISBN 0-9743201-0-2

To the Mississippi State family – past, present, and future.

CONTENTS

MSU ARCHIVES

MSU ARCHIVES

An artist's rendering of the first presidential home, 1880. The house was torn down in the 1960s to make room for Allen Hall.

PRESIDENTS RESIDENCE

Preceding pages:
The Bent of Tau Beta Pi monument has attracted students since it was erected in 1928 on the Drill Field. The larger photo was taken in 1971 and the smaller one in

PROVIDING OPPORTUNITY, SERVICE, AND LEADERSHIP FOR 125 years, Mississippi State University is rightfully proud of its history and reputation as "The People's University."

Much has changed since Governor John M. Stone signed the legislation organizing the Agricultural and Mechanical College of Mississippi February 28, 1878, but we continue to fulfill the promise that the founders envisioned. Their vision has matured into an accessible, responsive, and inclusive land-grant university that improves the lives of those it touches. Mississippi State graduates have helped change the face of the nation. Today's students and those who come tomorrow will continue that tradition, inspired by the achievements of the first 125 years.

A fascinating story unfolds in pictures on the following pages. The images recall the accomplishments, sacrifices, and day-to-day lives of the men and women who built the university.

Mississippi A&M was founded as one of the land-grant institutions authorized by the federal Morrill Act of 1862. After its creation by law in 1878, the college opened its doors to 354 students in fall 1880. The first president, Stephen D. Lee, led the college for nineteen years, operating with military-style discipline. The almost all-male student body wore uniforms, rose to reveille, attended chapel, and performed mandatory labor daily to help run the institution. The three buildings of the original campus were heated by coal-burning fireplaces and lighted with kerosene lamps.

The first graduates received their degrees in 1883. The first female graduated in 1888. Also in the 1880s, the Agricultural Experiment Station was created, the student newspaper began publishing, and the original dormitory evolved into Old Main, a campus centerpiece until it burned in 1959. The first football team took the field in 1895.

By 1900 the institution's annual budget was $193,000. Within a few years, Montgomery and Lee halls were built, the Maroon Band was performing, the Extension Service began taking practical knowledge to farmers and homemakers, and the forerunner of the national 4-H program was taking shape.

The Great War reduced enrollment to the extent that commencement was cancelled in 1917, but the campus provided a temporary home to about 800 Army technician trainees. The Great Depression came early to Mississippi, and the institution struggled financially.

Despite enormous difficulties, including Governor Theodore Bilbo's 1930 firing of the president and about one-third of the faculty and staff, the institution endured and progressed. After an absence

Dr. J. Charles Lee
became the seventeenth
president of Mississippi
State University
January 17, 2003,
after serving for one year
as interim president.
He formerly was vice
president for agriculture,
forestry, and veterinary
medicine and dean of the
College of Agriculture and
Life Sciences. From 1978
to 1983 he was dean of the
School of Forest Resources
and associate director
of the Mississippi
Agricultural and Forestry
Experiment Station.
His further administrative
experience was as vice
chancellor of the Texas
A&M University System
and as interim vice
president and provost for
Texas A&M University,
where he also headed the
Forest Science Department
and served within the
College of Agriculture and
Life Sciences and the Texas
Agricultural Experiment
Station. He earned a
bachelor's degree

in forest management and a doctorate in forestry/genetics from North Carolina State University, completing additional graduate work at Duke University. The U.S. Department of Agriculture Joint Council on Food and Agricultural Sciences, the Texas A&M Board of Regents, the Texas A&M College of Medicine, and the Mississippi Forestry Commission have honored Dr. Lee for outstanding service.

of almost twenty years, women were readmitted in 1930. Back in 1912, male students had protested a cadet's punishment for speaking to one of the few female students on campus. The ensuing ruckus brought the governor to campus to mediate and settle the dispute, but when the dust had settled, women students had been banished and the entire graduating class of 1913 demoted to private.

Mississippi A&M became Mississippi State College in 1932, and the transition into a modern university picked up speed. Enrollment had climbed to 2,500 by 1940, but World War II reduced student numbers to about 400 by D-Day. Still, the campus was busy, with thousands of military personnel and civilian workers receiving training. The postwar years brought a boom in enrollment and in new academic programs. The first doctoral degrees were awarded in the 1950s, and the university's research effort expanded greatly.

Mississippi State College became Mississippi State University in 1958. Enrollment topped 5,000 not long afterward, with about ten percent of the students being female.

The 1960s and 1970s brought dramatic changes. The university was integrated quietly and without incident in 1965. Less than a dozen years later, African Americans made up eleven percent of the student body, and more than one-third of students were women. Between 1961 and 1975, the portion of the faculty holding doctoral degrees grew from about one-third to more than two-thirds. The university stopped holding classes on Saturday, females were allowed to live off campus, and compulsory ROTC ended.

The 1980s and 1990s saw further rapid growth and the maturing of the university we know today. Mississippi State University now is the state's largest institution, with more than 16,600 students representing every county in Mississippi, every state in the nation, and many countries around the world. Almost half of the students are women, and eighteen percent of students are African Americans.

Today's institution both reflects its heritage and is energized by optimism about the future. Alumni, state policymakers, and constituents from all sectors of the population have sustained Mississippi State throughout its history. The university will continue to draw on that support as it aspires to new levels of achievement and even greater contributions to Mississippi, the nation, and the world in the next 125 years.

J. CHARLES LEE
June 2003

Snow falls on the presidential residence in 1999. Dr. William Giles and his family first occupied the home in the late 1960s.

125 YEARS AT MISSISSIPPI STATE UNIVERSITY

A PICTORIAL HISTORY OF THE PEOPLE'S UNIVERSITY

MSU ARCHIVES

Lee Hall burns October 20, 1948. The fire destroyed the roof and top floor, but firefighters were able to save the rest of the building.

Created in 1997 to honor donors to the Campaign for Mississippi State from 1992 to 1997, the Walk of Honor, *left*, has more than 6,400 permanent bricks.

Buildings make places, and places make for memories. Mississippi State affords many settings for a flood of memories. Some are framed within celebrated architecture, such as the cafeteria with its beautiful wooden trusses. Others are part of the landscape – the pasture where cows grazed near the baseball field or the Drill Field. No graduate ever left without at least one memory, whether a sanctioned university event or a prank, of the Drill Field, a magnet for celebration.

Comparing the aerial views from 1953 and 2003 dramatizes the physical growth of the campus. About one new building a year has been added for the last twenty-five. The memories, though, cannot be measured, nor the spirit of Mississippi State captured in a photo. Imagine George Hall as an infirmary and the sadness within its walls after nineteen-year-old students died of influenza. Revisit the horror of the Old Main fire – the shock of seeing its hull after the conflagration. Think of the days when the Textile Building could be viewed all the way from the front of Montgomery Hall or when railroad tracks ran through the campus. Relive the whimsy of Malfunction Junction's "Don't Never Ever Enter" marker. The setting is an important stage for memories of people who touch our lives. No stage is richer than Mississippi State's campus. Some of the landmarks on the next pages are places we never knew, but the stories are so real, and the photographs so plentiful, the images have become a part of our collective consciousness.

Thomas Jefferson had a vision for an "academical village" when he planned the University of Virginia. He conceived a community where architecture and academic life would be inseparable, where place would be part of the student culture, where the rituals of academic life would settle on those present and accompany them for the rest of their lives. Certainly Mississippi State's vision is no less lofty and its setting no less memorable to those who have come here and found the inspiration for a life of work, service, and learning that need not stop with graduation. These agglomerated buildings, from the eclectic Bowen Hall to the ever-lit Architecture Building to the sleek, curvy new Hunter Henry Center, all have their stories to tell. Take a look; remember their stories and your own; and anticipate the stories of those who will follow you.

Mississippi State architecture graduate Janet Smith is known for her planning and development of Oriole Park at Camden Yards in Baltimore, where she leads redevelopment of abandoned or underutilized downtown areas. She currently is evaluating renovation of Fenway Park in Boston and has participated in developing ideas for the World Trade Center site in New York.

Michael Fazio, A.I.A, an architect, architectural historian, and author, teaches in the MSU College of Architecture. He holds a bachelor's degree from Auburn University, a master's from Ohio State University, and a doctorate from Cornell University. He practices architecture in the Southeast, most often consulting in documentary and forensic architectural preservation.

JANET MARIE SMITH & MICHAEL FAZIO

FRED FAULK

Cadets drill while spectators watch from the steps of the Old Academic Building in this 1904 view of the campus. The Chemistry Building also is visible, *left*, and the towers of the Textile Building soar in the distance.

MSU ARCHIVES

Most of the first buildings on campus, including the original Chemistry Building, *right*, were Gothic in design and featured a spire or two. This 1904 photograph also shows the building's addition, *left*.

MSU ARCHIVES

Distinguished by its twin towers, the Industrial Education Building, originally named the Textile Building, is one of three campus buildings on the National Register of Historic Places. Built in 1900, the Italianate structure housed the Textile School, where students trained to make a variety of products, including fabrics from cotton and wool.

FRED FAULK

The view from Allen Hall across the Drill Field to Lee Hall

RUSS HOUSTON

The lines and angles suggest a setting appropriate to the Architectural Library, but the location is actually the fourth floor of the Mitchell Memorial Library, the main library on campus. The photo was shot from the James H. Carr Phi Delta Kappa Undergraduate Study Room.

FRED FAULK

FRED FAULK

Before its extensive expansion and renovation in the mid 1990s, Mitchell Memorial Library was distinguished by the "Tree of Life" iron sculpture that hung from the third floor.

FRED FAULK

Imitation is the sincerest form of flattery. In contributing funds for a new building, Dave C. Swalm requested that designers replicate his personal favorite, Lee Hall. The Swalm Chemical Engineering Building provides a mirror image to Lee, even though the two were constructed ninety-one years apart. The state-of-the-art Swalm Building opened in 2000.

FRED FAULK

A souvenir plate from the 1950s features Lee Hall in the center and other campus buildings around the rim.

MSU ARCHIVES

Constructed in 1909 as an academic building and chapel, the Beaux Arts-style Lee Hall is named for Stephen D. Lee, first president. It houses offices of the dean of students, vice president for student affairs, enrollment services, orientation, telecommunications, *Mississippi Quarterly*, the Society for the Study of Southern Literature, and the English and Foreign Languages departments.

Old Main, built in 1880 and expanded over several years, housed cadets and was reputed to be the country's largest dormitory under one roof.

MSU ARCHIVES

Flames light up the sky as Old Main dormitory for men burns January 22, 1959. The fire claimed the life of one of the dorm's 1,100 residents.

MSU ARCHIVES

To honor all who
lived in Old Main during
its seventy-nine years
of existence, the bricks
from the dormitory were
used to build the
Chapel of Memories.

The future looks bright at the Hunter Henry Center, home to the Alumni Association, the MSU Foundation, and the office of external affairs. Alumnus Hunter W. Henry, Jr., class of 1950, a resident of San Marcos, Texas, made the cornerstone commitment of $3 million toward the 41,000 square-foot facility, which was dedicated in spring 2003.

Blooming Oriental
Pears frame the
interdenominational
Chapel of Memories
in this 1990s photograph.
The chapel has been
the site of weddings,
memorial services,
and other events since
the 1970s. Its carillon
plays every hour.

FRED FAULK

MSU ARCHIVES

Students pause for a
photo in front of the
Old Chapel in 1910.

FRED FAULK

The design of the main
building on the MSU
Meridian campus evokes
the Chapel of Memories.

The cafeteria on a snowy day in the 1940s. Built in 1923 to support Old Main residence hall, the cafeteria could serve 1,000 students at one time. It later was named for George Perry of the class of 1919.

MSU ARCHIVES

Students ate in this dining room in the early 1900s, before the cafeteria was built.

MSU ARCHIVES

Milk and military science: the Dairy and ROTC building

MSU ARCHIVES

George Hall housed the campus infirmary when thirty-seven students died in the 1918 influenza epidemic. The building later was converted to other uses.

MSU ARCHIVES

The Cooley Building, physical plant headquarters, appears on the National Register of Historic Places.

Originally named the John M. Stone Cotton Mills, the 1902 structure was a textile mill for Starkville. The university

purchased it in 1966 and renamed it for Earle Edward Cooley, a 1910 graduate and former superintendent of the

utilities and power maintenance plant. A Bulldog adorns the base of the tower.

27

FRED FAULK

Looking across
Chadwick Lake to the
Bryan Athletic
Administration Building,
right, and the
Joe Frank Sanderson
Center.

Blooming flowers
brighten the sign
that greets entrants
to the campus.

FRED FAULK

Limestone columns
that once graced the
front of Atlanta's Union
Station now tower in
front of the Cobb
Institute of Archaeology.
A $1.2-million gift by
Cully (class of 1909) and
Lois Cobb established
the institute.

FRED FAULK

Eckie's Pond, the oldest landmark on campus, is named for A.B. McKay, the horticulture professor responsible for digging a permanent pool to supply water to greenhouses and other structures in the late 1800s. McKay's nickname, Echo, became Eckie through the years.

FRED FAULK

A 1916 bird's-eye view of the horticulture grounds.

MSU ARCHIVES

The Mississippi State College cornerstone is in the middle of the one remaining column of the pair that marked the entrance to the campus.

MSU ARCHIVES

A 2003 aerial view reveals the growth and development on the campus. McCool Hall and the Colvard Union occupy the site where Old Main once was.

FRED FAULK

A 1953 aerial view of the campus. The Old Main dormitory dominates one side of the Drill Field. The President's House stands in the middle of President's Circle. The city of Starkville is to the west, *top left.*

MSU ARCHIVES

South Farm at sunset.

Early risers on South
Farm at dawn.

Aerial view of South
Farm. The catfish ponds
facilitate a variety of
other projects, including
raising freshwater shrimp
and striped bass.

Architecture students
enjoy a break outside
Giles Hall.

FRED FAULK

FRED FAULK

The Wise Center is
home to the University
Television Center,
the Department of
Animal and Dairy Sciences,
the Animal Health Center,
and the College of
Veterinary Medicine,
which was founded in 1978
and is today one of only
twenty-seven accredited
veterinary colleges in the
United States.

FRED FAULK

Bowen Hall, built in 1929,
is listed as a Mississippi
Landmark. Portions of
the Industrial Education
Building, *right*, and
the power plant, *left*,
can also be seen.

MSU ARCHIVES

The "Don't Never Ever
Enter" sign from the
1960s is gone, but
Malfunction Junction still
lives up to its name.

Cresswell residence hall,
renovated in 2002, bears
the MSU seal.

PAUL W. GRIMES

34

RUSS HOUSTON

The Joe Frank Sanderson Center, with the Department of Recreational Sports, is one of the largest buildings on campus and sits across the lake from the Bryan Athletic Administration Building.

Humphrey Coliseum, home court for the men's and women's basketball teams, was completed in 1974. The 11,000-seat arena has hosted superstar entertainers, including Bruce Springsteen, Garth Brooks, and Tina Turner.

FRED FAULK

Building the gymnasium in 1950. The gym was later named for James H. "Babe" McCarthy, who coached men's basketball teams to SEC championships in the early 1960s. Because Mississippi collegiate teams were not allowed to play racially integrated teams at the time, McCarthy secured permission from President Dean Colvard to take the 1963 squad to the NCAA tournament. They lost by ten points to Chicago's Loyola University, an integrated team.

MSU ARCHIVES

35

MSU ARCHIVES

A history professor lectures to his class in 1913.

They're history. Wooden desks, like those inside Montgomery Hall in the 1990s, *left*, are no longer used in classrooms.

Mississippi State University faculty have always placed high value on teaching and learning. That emphasis is an integral part of our mission, with learning included in the university's official seal. Eight faculty, including President Stephen D. Lee, were listed in the first catalog of Mississippi A&M, published in 1880. By 2002 the Mississippi State faculty ranks had increased to more than 900. During the institution's 125-year history and its continued growth, one thing has remained constant: the faculty commitment to teaching and to integrating research into classroom experiences to enhance the learning process for our students.

A very personal example illustrates the importance of teaching at our university. As a student, I was one of very few women in my first physics class at Mississippi State. Mr. Clifford Rose, my first physics teacher at the university, became one of my favorite teachers in spite of the fact I initially lived in fear of his calling on me in class. Years later I faced a much more diverse class in that same classroom in Hilbun Hall – not as a student but as a faculty member. In my own career, Mississippi State has done far more than provide a first-rate education as a foundation. Outstanding teachers and mentors have encouraged me and other young faculty members to maintain the highest teaching standards throughout a career.

The value that Mississippi State places on teaching is seen in generous alumni support recognizing faculty contributions to generations of students. The Alumni Association awards for teaching, research, and service; the John Grisham Master Teacher Awards; the Grisham Faculty Excellence Awards; and the Grisham Teaching Excellence Awards are tangible reminders that Mississippi State has defined quality undergraduate instruction as one of its hallmarks throughout its history.

The ways that faculty members provide instruction may have changed in 125 years, but the core values of the institution continue. Dr. Buz Walker, mathematics instructor and president for five years, could not have foreseen the use of technology in the classroom or the availability of online courses. But he and a host of highly regarded professors over the years – Dr. William Flowers Hand and Dr. Clyde Sheely of chemistry, Dr. John K. Bettersworth of history, Dr. August Raspet of aerophysics, and countless others – would certainly recognize and applaud the dedication of Mississippi State faculty in providing our students with quality learning experiences. That commitment is one of our lasting legacies.

SANDRA HARPOLE

Dr. Sandra Harpole, interim associate vice president for research and director of the Center for Science, Mathematics, and Technology, is a graduate of Mississippi State University, having received her doctorate in education in 1986. A former high school physics and chemistry teacher, she has been a member of the physics faculty at Mississippi State since 1987. She has generated more than $4.3 million in research funding, has been recognized as Outstanding Faculty Woman, and was honored with the Alumni Association Faculty Achievement Award for her contributions in service. Among the teaching awards Dr. Harpole has received at both the high school and university levels are the Presidential Award for Excellence in Science Teaching and the John Grisham Master Teacher Award.

FRED FAULK

MSU ARCHIVES

A sophomore textiles class, 1902. Established in 1899, the Textiles Department provided instruction in the theoretical and practical aspects of cotton manufacturing. Textiles ceased to be offered as a major in 1914.

The *First Annual Catalogue of the Agricultural and Mechanical College of Mississippi* appeared for the 1880–1881 school year.

The *Mississippi State University Bulletin* today is a 340-page publication that is updated annually and available online.

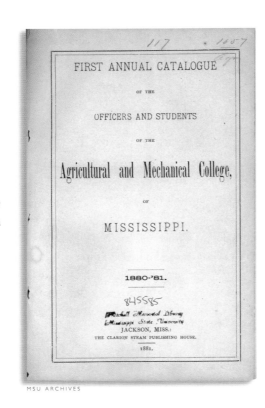

MSU ARCHIVES

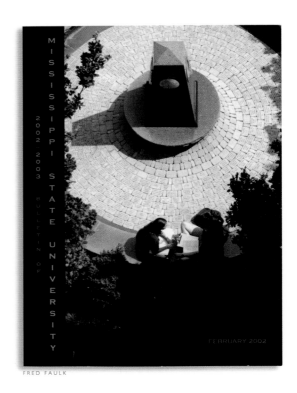

FRED FAULK

"Feet flat on the floor, and don't look at the keys." Students in a 1953 typing class work on words per minute.

MSU ARCHIVES

A.B. McKay, professor of horticulture, demonstrates the proper technique for splitting ferns.

MSU ARCHIVES

On their best behavior. Students enrolled in a 1970s social usage class put their skills to the test at a reception with Dr. and Mrs. William Giles. Dr. Giles was the thirteenth president of the university.

MSU ARCHIVES

39

Engineering students strike a pose with their surveying equipment. The Old Academic Building and Old Main dormitory are visible in the background.

MSU ARCHIVES

Surveying, 1990s style. Engineering students practice on the Drill Field. Lee Hall and the Union are in the background.

FRED FAULK

"Smartboards" have replaced many chalkboards, and computers and projectors are found in many of today's classrooms.

RUSS HOUSTON

RUSS HOUSTON

Architecture students sit in the atrium of Giles Hall, working on projects on their laptop computers.

FRED FAULK

RUSS HOUSTON

Paint to pixels. Art majors choose their media based on their plans for a future in fine arts or graphic design.

An engineering professor teaches on-site students and remote students simultaneously in his distance education class.

Learning by doing.
A 1940s agricultural
education class learns to
teach farm mechanics
by using the "hands-on"
method.

MSU ARCHIVES

MSU COLLEGE OF EDUCATION

From the College of
Education to the grade
school classroom.
Student teaching is the
culminating field
experience in the teacher
preparation program.

A student in the School of
Forest Resources, 1972,
is knee deep in knowledge
of the habitats and lives
of wildlife.

MSU ARCHIVES

Archaeology students learn to properly excavate and identify minerals, rocks, and other objects on a dig during summer session, 1969.

The cow with the window stomach is a favorite of school children, who get a close look at agriculture when they visit the campus. A staff member explains the cow's digestive system during a College of Veterinary Medicine open house in the 1980s.

Labwork is an integral part of many science classes.

FRED FAULK

A biology student places a specimen under a microscope for a closer look.

FRED FAULK

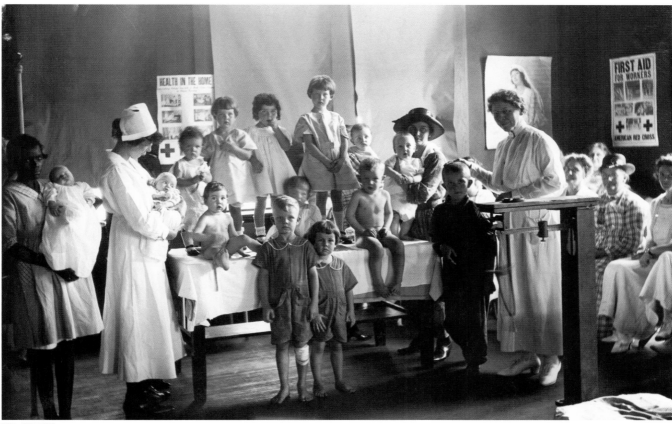

MSU ARCHIVES

A healthy learning
environment.
Mothers and children
visit A&M College
for a child health-related
short course in 1920.

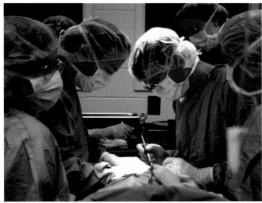

TOM THOMPSON

Veterinary medicine
students observe faculty
members perform surgery
on one of the more than
6,000 pets that are
treated each year at the
Animal Health Center.
The students get practical
experience in treating
both domestic and exotic
animals.

A tiger from the Jackson,
Mississippi, zoo receives
anesthesia through the
blue tube as veterinary
medicine students, staff,
and faculty prepare to
take X-rays.

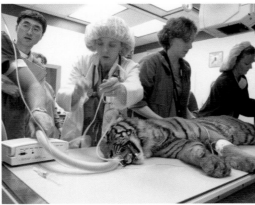

TOM THOMPSON

The coed class of 1913 would be the last for a while. After a female and male student were found talking in the library, cadets were forbidden to visit with the coeds "for the purpose of social conversation or study." The ensuing protest resulted in many cadets being expelled and women banned from enrollment until 1930.

Females were in the minority for much of the university's existence. This was probably the entire female population in 1898. Women students boarded with relatives and others who opened their homes in Starkville or with faculty families.

The thirteen members of the Mississippi A&M Class of 1883 hailed from places like Horn Lake, Aberdeen, Macon, Buena Vista, and Starkville. The photograph was taken in April 1881.

Registration the
old-fashioned way.
Students pack into the
Animal Husbandry
Building, where they fill
out cards for each of their
classes in the 1960s.

MSU ARCHIVES

MSU ARCHIVES

From standing in line
to registering online.
The first computerized
registration in 1969
causes long lines –
something today's
students cannot fathom
as they schedule courses
from their personal
computers.

By the 1990s, regular exercise was part of many students' routines. Aerobics and a number of physical education classes are offered in the Joe Frank Sanderson Center, which is equipped with basketball and racquetball courts and a swimming pool.

FRED FAULK

The work of the Division of College Extension spread from the campus to county fairs. An exhibit that won first place at the fair in Wiggins is displayed in the Gulfport City Hall in 1914.

MSU ARCHIVES

Which way to the runway? A Style Dress Revue at the 1935 State Club Congress.

MSU ARCHIVES

MSU ARCHIVES

Engineering a break. Students enjoy free time between classes outside Carpenter Hall in the late 1970s. Many engineering classes are still taught in the building.

A student uses a ledger and typewriter as she completes her accounting homework in the 1970s.

MSU ARCHIVES

Students check out books from the library in 1951. The stairs to the closed stacks can be seen in the background. Only staff were allowed to enter the stacks to retrieve the material.

MSU ARCHIVES

Which came first?
Junior high school
4-H students consider
egg yolks as part of a
project in the 1990s.

As a community
service in the 1970s,
the Industrial Education
Club repairs items
collected from the
Starkville Junior League
for distribution to the
needy at Christmas.

MSU ARCHIVES

Self-promotion.
Delegates to a 1930
Mississippi 4-H Club
Congress line up in front
of Carpenter Hall.

MSU ARCHIVES

Commencement
ceremonies have been
held in the football
stadium, Lee Hall,
the Animal Husbandry
Building, Humphrey
Coliseum, and on the
Drill Field. At one time,
commencements lasted
up to four days.
Commencement
ceremonies currently
are held in December
and May.

Early economists. The President's Report for 1913–1915 included a summary of Markets and Rural Economics, "the study of rural surveys, social centers, leaderships, intellectual ideals, economic conveniences, communications, and transportation," among other things.

MSU ARCHIVES

Attendees listen to a program on home hygiene, including instruction on caring for the sick, at a 1925 4-H Club Congress.

MSU ARCHIVES

Army Lt. General Troy Middleton (Ret.), class of 1909, addresses commencement during the 1950s. Middleton held the highest rank of Mississippi State alumni who served in World War II. He was a member of General Dwight Eisenhower's staff and later was the fifteenth president of Louisiana State University.

MSU ARCHIVES

MSU ARCHIVES

Commencement is held on the Drill Field in 1923.

FRED FAULK

President George Herbert Walker Bush, commencement speaker in 1989, holds a fan in a light moment with Dr. Donald Zacharias.

Dr. Clyde Q. Sheely, demigod of freshman chemistry for nearly forty years, leads the processional as mace bearer for the May 28, 1972, commencement, as he did for many others.

FRED FAULK

MSU president W.L. Giles caps a graduate in 1969.

MSU ARCHIVES

MSU ARCHIVES

This Mechanic Arts diploma was awarded in 1895 and signed by each faculty member.

NANCY BARDWELL

The presentation may have changed – diplomas are now encased in leather – and the size of the graduating class grown, but today's graduates likely feel the same sense of accomplishment and relief their nineteenth century predecessors experienced.

Good, not-so-clean fun.
A student skimboards in
2002 on the Drill Field,
left. In 1969 students
skimboard in front
of the Pi Kappa Alpha
fraternity house, where
the amphitheater
eventually would be
built. The rest of
fraternity row did not
exist at the time.

I grew up in Starkville, convinced that nothing of this world was quite as good as Mississippi State University. I came by it honestly. My Daddy came here as a student in 1969. Four degrees, a long stint as a professor, and more than a quarter of a century later, he can still be seen walking with his head held high across the Drill Field. Like me, he remains convinced that nothing of this world is quite as good as Mississippi State.

He came by that honestly, too. My Granddaddy hitched a ride from Union County down to "old State College" toward the end of the Great Depression. He found a new home in Old Main, which was located in the center of a growing campus. That was convenient for Pa Paw and his classmates, all ROTC cadets who would learn to be soldiers on what they called the Parade Ground. Shortly after Granddaddy finished in 1941, he was commissioned into the Army and served with many of his classmates through World War II. After the war, he came back to Mississippi, where he eventually became the county agent in Jasper County and raised my father. He made sure his only child understood just how special this place was.

I guess you could say that I didn't even choose Mississippi State when I finished high school in 1999. It had chosen me long before I was born. By the time I arrived as a student, a fire had destroyed the old dormitory that had meant so much to my Granddaddy. Though some of my classmates still drilled along the grassy center of campus that we knew as the Drill Field, most of us just walked along this beaten path of history. In the distance, bells could be heard marking the hour. It is only fitting that the chapel from which the bells tolled was built from the remains of the old dormitory in which we might have lived had history dealt a different hand. Somehow, I think it is in this scene that the story of all of us is told. So much has changed, and so much remains the same. My experiences as a student would only slightly resemble those of my father and my grandfather. Still, I share something with a unique group of about 100,000 scattered around the globe – something that is easier felt than described. The passing of time has endowed us with different experiences, yet somehow in the present and the future we find the past. If I could place all of the experiences and actors on those hallowed grounds, it wouldn't be hard at all for me to explain why there is nothing of this world quite as good as Mississippi State.

PARKER WISEMAN

*Parker Wiseman,
a 2003 graduate of
Mississippi State University,
was a recipient of the
John C. Stennis Scholarship
for Public Service.
Throughout his college
career, he was an active
student leader, serving as
the Student Association
vice president and
president. Among his
proudest achievements
was being selected
Mr. MSU by his peers.*

A. & M. College, Mississippi.

Dear Sir: JUL 27 1923

We have received your certificate of credits from the _McComb_ High School. The units carried by the certificate are sufficient for your admission. We shall be glad to have you enter the next session, September _19_, 192_3_.

Yours truly,

J J Waddell

Chairman, Entrance Committee.

Imagine the anticipation the recipient of this postcard felt in 1923 upon being notified that he had been accepted to A&M. The card was his entrance ticket and, in effect, a passport from his hometown of McComb, in the southwestern part of the state, to life on a college campus in northeast Mississippi.

Heavy snow in the 1959–1960 school year prompted students to try sledding down a hill. Because snow rarely falls, they had very little practice.

Not all bras were burned in the 1970s. This one was confiscated during a freshman panty raid on a women's residence hall in 1980. Today's fraternities are more likely to conduct "pantry raids," in which they collect canned food for the disadvantaged.

THE FRESHMAN CHRISTMAS REPORT

It is a tradition here at State for all Freshmen (skin-heads, that is) to learn verbatim the following report and be ready, willing, and able to recite it by the first day of December, 1948. The report is as follows:

Sirs:

Realizing with exhuberance the unimpeded passage of time which unhaltingly brings near this glad and festive Yuletide season, it is my paramount wish and uncontrollable desire that, I, freshman (your complete name), be permitted to make the following report:

On this ___ hour of the ___ day of December, nineteen hundrd and forty-eight anno domini, there remain but ___ days, hours, and ___ minutes, until we shall be allowed to desist from our fatiguing labors at this institution of higher learning and proceed cum magna celeritate to our respective domiciles, mine being located in the town of ___, the county of ___, and the state of ___. Thank you, sirs.

(Time will be figured to twelve noon December 18, 1948.)

There was a time when all freshmen, or "skinheads," were expected to recite the Freshman Christmas Report verbatim upon request, or command, by an upperclassman. During meals, a freshman could be asked to stand on a cafeteria table and say the report without any errors, filling in – to the exact minute – how much time was left in the semester before the Christmas break. The tradition, popular for many years, ended in the late 1960s. The report, _above_, is from the 1948–1949 Student Handbook.

Inspiring creativity, inviting trouble. From the time it was erected in the middle of the Drill Field, the bust of the first president, General Stephen D. Lee, has inspired student shenanigans. A group of friends hangs out with the General in 1971, and another foursome adorns the statue with hat and umbrella in 1977.

MSU ARCHIVES

MSU ARCHIVES

Somehow, it looks more serious in black and white: A 1930s pillow fight in an Old Main room.

MSU ARCHIVES

Sororities and fraternities
host trick-or-treaters,
and the Campus
Activities Board sponsors
a carnival each year to
provide a safe Halloween
option for local children.
Proceeds benefit
community charities.

RAYMOND BROOKS

International students
enjoy cricket on the Drill
Field in 2003. The wicket
is below the statue of
President Stephen D. Lee
as the bowler awaits
the pitch.

PAUL W. GRIMES

FRED FAULK

Spring always brings students out to sit beneath the Oriental Magnolia on the Drill Field, and 2002 was no exception.

PAUL W. GRIMES

MSU ARCHIVES

Frank Adams of Okolona, Mississippi, noted in his 1917–1918 Student Handbook that he was a sophomore and belonged to the Chickasaw County Club.

The games may change, but students will always pass time by playing on the Drill Field. A student uses her cell phone to entertain herself in 2003.

Remember crinolines?
Full-skirted formals were
all the rage for females at
this 1950s junior-senior
dance in the cafeteria.

MSU ARCHIVES

Lambda Chi Alpha
fraternity brothers
unwind with a
little foosball action
in the 1970s.

MSU ARCHIVES

MSU ARCHIVES

Dognap. A weary student
and visitor catch a few
winks one sleepy day in
1964. The bench was a
gift to the university from
the class of 1926.

Two roommates don't seem to mind the mess or cigarette smoke in their Sessums room in 1970. Sessums today is a female residence hall.

MSU ARCHIVES

A student adjusts her television set manually before the days of the TV remote control. Note the cassette player and clock radio on her bookshelves. Today's students are more likely to have compact discs, MP3 players, and digital clocks.

MSU ARCHIVES

Moving into a residence hall can be a slow process. Students and their parents frequently must wait in line to get into buildings.

FRED FAULK

FRED FAULK

A 1990s campus resident makes the most of her space.

Styles change, but laundry is a constant, as this 1990 photo reminds.

FRED FAULK

Flags in Perry Cafeteria represent the home states and countries of students who have attended MSU.

FRED FAULK

FRED FAULK

No place to count calories. State Fountain sells baked goods, MSU cheese, ice cream, milk, and coffee, making it a tempting place to take a break in 1988.

MSU ARCHIVES

Campus food these days includes fast food from nationally branded chains such as Wendy's, Chick-fil-A and Subway.

Students in the 1950s pick up their dry cleaning at Roberts Laundry, named for its former manager. After more than 100 years of service to the campus, the laundry closed in 2003.

Campus politics reached a fever pitch in the 1970s. Students line up in Colvard Union to vote for their favorite Student Government Association candidates.

Many students were
called to active duty in
World War II. Those left
on campus helped
support the United States
by selling and buying
bonds from 1941 to 1945.

MSU ARCHIVES

Prior to 1972,
the minimum voting
age was twenty-one.
Students who were old
enough to vote in national
and state elections cast
their ballots outside
the YMCA in 1948.

MSU ARCHIVES

Two days after the
September 11, 2001,
terrorist attacks on
Washington, D.C.,
and New York City,
students gather for a
somber candlelight vigil
to honor the victims.

FRED FAULK

FRED FAULK

The American flag is backlit by the setting sun one day in the 1990s as university police officers lower the flag on the Drill Field. McCool Hall is in the background.

FRED FAULK

Fall's nip in the air and turning leaves are always welcome after the stifling heat of a Mississippi summer.

Ready for the Rebels. A police officer directs traffic on Lee Boulevard as the campus prepares for a football game against archrival, the University of Mississippi, in the 1960s. Signs read, "Ole Miss Reeks" and "Stick the Rebels."

MSU ARCHIVES

There are all kinds of ways to show school spirit, as a student demonstrates for homecoming in 1973.

MSU ARCHIVES

FRED FAULK

Beauty is in the eye of the fan beholding Bully, the official MSU mascot. TaTonka Gold, an American Kennel Club-registered English bulldog, is Bully XIX, as of 2001.

FRED FAULK

Too much spirit? Campus police "arrest" the human Bully mascot in the 1970s.

MSU ARCHIVES

Jack-o'-lanterns to Christmas trees, bumper stickers to neckties, one never knows where Bully will appear next, as this pumpkin proves in 1987.

A sorority participates in the 1992 Derby Day, a national event held on many college campuses.

FRED FAULK

Sometimes it's hard to tell who enjoys MSU more – students or their parents.

Getting a taste of university life. High school students bob for apples during a Discovery Day in the 1970s. Discovery Days encourage potential MSU students and their families to visit colleges and schools and attend campus events, such as football games, academic fairs, and concerts.

MSU ARCHIVES

Some things never change. Students walk on the Drill Field as they change classes in 1973 and 2003.

MSU ARCHIVES

PAUL W. GRIMES

Timeless silhouette. A couple share an umbrella and a kiss in the 1980s.

FRED FAULK

MSU BOOKSTORE

In other words,
"My kid's a Dawg."

MSU ARCHIVES

Three telephone
operators work the
switchboard, handling
incoming and outgoing
calls, in the 1950s.

The influx of GIs returning
from World War II in the
1940s necessitated
temporary student housing,
known as Hardy City.

MSU ARCHIVES

The *Reflector* staff was mostly male until the 1970s. Staff members in 1936 wear coats, ties, and hats. By 1968, the changes are obvious: no hats.

The November 1892 issue of the *College Reflector* and the March 25, 2003, issue of the *Reflector* campus newspaper. The periodical began as the *Dialectic Star* in 1883, a monthly containing college news and essays on "educational, literary, and industrial" subjects. The student newspaper currently publishes twice a week, on Tuesdays and Fridays.

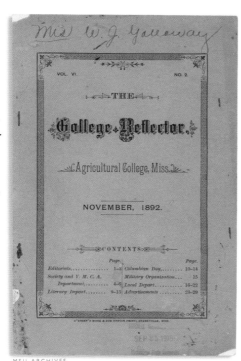

A member of the Skydiving Club free falls for ninety-five seconds, grinning all the while. Active in 1966, when the photo was taken, the Skydiving Club has gone the way of organizations such as the Turkey Snatchers, 1908; The Dip and Strike Club, devoted to geology and geography, 1949; the Lion Tamer's Club, 1923; the Farm Equipment Club, 1956; and the Spirit of America, 1985. Approximately 296 organizations currently are registered on campus.

Students have access to several labs on campus, such as this one in the library, where they check e-mail, type papers, run programs, design Web pages, and perform a variety of other computer-related tasks.

FRED FAULK

Students examine the cockpit of a biplane in front of Lee Hall in or about 1917.

MSU ARCHIVES

Most students
belonged to one or
more extracurricular
groups in the early
years of the university.
The Horticultural Society,
shown in 1925,
is now called the
Horticulture Club and
is one of the oldest
surviving organizations.

MSU ARCHIVES

The power of pizza.
Free food can be a strong
enticement for students
to participate in
extracurricular activities,
such as this chapter
meeting of the Golden
Key International
Honor Society.

PAUL W. GRIMES

Cadets parade in 1911. The Textile and Chemistry buildings are in the background.

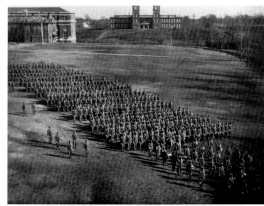

MSU ARCHIVES

MSU ARCHIVES

Cadets participate in a military dress parade in the 1970s.

Dancing to the sounds
of a big band, students
attend a military ball
during the 1940s.

MSU ARCHIVES

A cadet's Mississippi
A&M pin from the early
1900s, *top*, and the
crossed-rifles pin cadets
wore in the late 1800s.

MSU ARCHIVES

79

The George Rifles Club
performs a demonstration
in 1907 in front of
Old Main.

MSU ARCHIVES

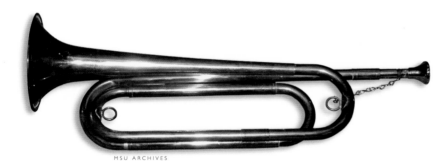

MSU ARCHIVES

A bugle remains from
the years when cadets
played reveille and taps
at the beginning and
end of the day.

As cadets, students
were required to wear
uniforms until 1930.

MSU ARCHIVES

Brass buttons secured the cadet uniform jacket.

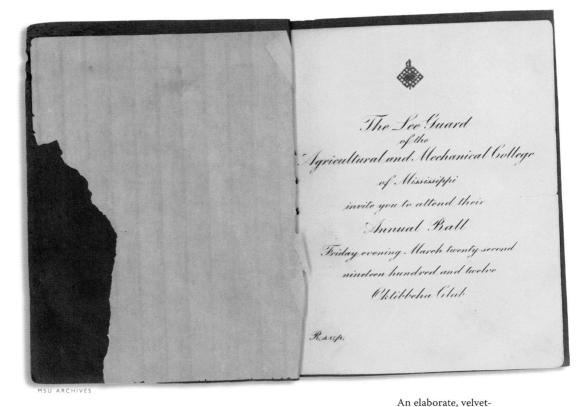

The Lee Guard
of the
Agricultural and Mechanical College
of Mississippi
invite you to attend their
Annual Ball
Friday evening March twenty-second
nineteen hundred and twelve
Oktibbeha Club

R.s.v.p.

A Mississippi A&M cadet's eagle pin.

An elaborate, velvet-bound invitation to the Lee Guard Ball reveals the prestige of the organization. The elite group drilled in precision and represented the college in memorials or other events. Lee Guard was a forerunner to fraternities, which were not allowed at the time.

81

Cadets train on the
Drill Field in 1958, *top*,
and 1948.

MSU ARCHIVES

MSU ARCHIVES

ROTC students stand at attention in the 1980s. ROTC was required of all male students until 1969. Nationally, women were allowed in the Army ROTC program in 1972.

MSU ARCHIVES

A 1940s Army personnel training unit conducts a war training exercise during World War II.

MSU ARCHIVES

The Famous Maroon
Band holds one of its
many practices on the
band field behind the
Industrial Education
Building in the 1990s.

FRED FAULK

Students, faculty, and
staff enjoy a performance
by the Concert Band in
front of Colvard Union
in the 1990s.

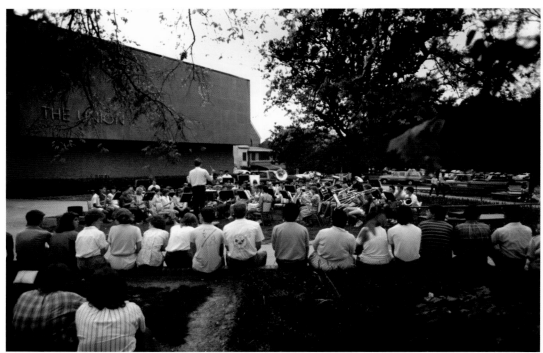

FRED FAULK

MSU ARCHIVES

The insignia for a student
lettering in band.

MSU ARCHIVES

MSU ARCHIVES

The 1926 Famous Forty
Band stands proudly
behind the Meridian
Football Underwriters
Trophy they won
October 9, 1926.

All forty members of the
1926 Famous Forty Band
signed the photograph of
the trophy they earned.

MSU ARCHIVES

An A&M Cadet
Band member writes
home in 1908.

One famous Tupelo, Mississippian, interviews another. Jack Cristil, "The Voice of the Bulldogs" for more than fifty years, takes a time out from announcing football and basketball games to talk with Elvis Presley, who was also just getting started in the 1950s.

MSU ARCHIVES

MSU ARCHIVES

Fannie Lou Hamer, civil rights pioneer and native Mississippian, speaks to the Afro-American Club in 1969.

Senator John C. Stennis, who served in the U.S. Senate for forty-one years, crowns the homecoming queen in 1973. Stennis was an alumnus of MSU, where he served as a cheerleader.

FRED FAULK

Homecoming queens wore this one-of-a-kind crown during the 1950s and 1960s.

MSU ARCHIVES

World famous billiards
player Willie Mosconi
plays an exhibition match
against an MSU freshman
in the 1970s, one in a
series of such events that
brought celebrities to
campus.

The man who would be
president. Jimmy Carter
dons an MSU hat while
visiting campus during
his 1976 presidential
campaign.

Comedian Bob Hope,
right, performed on
campus in 1976.

Best-selling author
John Grisham visits his
alma mater in the 1990s.

RUSS HOUSTON

Ranked No. 3 in
the world in 1989,
Andre Agassi practices
on the Pitts Tennis
Courts while on campus
to visit friends.

RUSS HOUSTON

MSU ARCHIVES

A vintage Alumni
Association sticker
sent to members.

MSU ARCHIVES

The train was the main
form of transportation for
students at the turn of
the twentieth century.
Passenger service ended
in 1950 and freight service
in 1969. The tracks that
ran through the middle
of campus were removed
about ten years later.
The John C. Stennis
Institute of Government
is located in the
former depot.

Even before students
had cars, they liked to go
away for the weekends,
giving MSU its reputation
as a "suitcase campus."
Students wait for the bus
in this 1930s photograph.

MSU ARCHIVES

Luggage is piled atop
the Yazoo to Clarksdale
bus that transported
many students to and
from campus in the 1930s.

MSU ARCHIVES

Public service has long been a responsibility of fraternity and sorority members. Members of the Lambda Chi Alpha fraternity pick up litter along Highway 82 east to Columbus in 1969.

Pi Kappa Alpha became the first fraternity on campus in the late 1920s. Previously, it was illegal in Mississippi for universities and colleges to allow fraternal organizations. The Pike house, built in 1951, also was the first Greek house on campus.

"An Engineer with Designs" is the theme of the civil engineering float, pulled by a tractor in a 1951 parade.

MSU ARCHIVES

Alumni and professors from the classes of 1891–1925 pose for a group photo at the Mississippi State College seventy-fifth anniversary in 1953.

Students celebrate the centennial of MSU on Proclamation Day, February 28, 1978, in Humphrey Coliseum.

MSU ARCHIVES

MSU ATHLETIC MEDIA RELATIONS

Center Erick Dampier, *left,* was named first-team, All-SEC in back-to-back seasons (1995–1996 and 1996–1997). A member of MSU's 1996 Final Four team, Dampier has enjoyed a successful career in the NBA since his years as a Bulldog.

Bailey Howell, *above,* first Mississippi State All-American athlete, basketball. Howell won many awards and accolades in his college and professional basketball careers. He has been inducted into the Mississippi, MSU, and NBA Basketball Halls of Fame.

I became a part of Mississippi State University in 1953. It had taken me twenty-eight years and a lot of turns in the road to come to this place I know as home today. Fortunately, it didn't take nearly so long for Mississippi State to become a part of me.

Little did I know as I sat in athletic director Dudy Noble's office that day so many years ago, not only was I being offered the opportunity to broadcast athletic events for Mississippi State, I was forming a bond that would last a lifetime. I was a sports broadcaster looking for a place to do play-by-play; the university sought someone to tell its athletic story. What we both found was a relationship – a friendship – launched by verbal agreement but as steadfast as if inked in blood.

For Mississippi State, and for any university, athletics, of course, is a showcase. It is the mechanism by which the university can reach out and sell itself on a local, regional, and even national scale, reaching the widest audience. It is a window to the world. Athletics communicates with alumni of the institution, fans across the country, and the general public unlike any other area of the campus. It touches the emotions of people from all walks of life. At Mississippi State, athletics does all of this in the Mississippi State way – with pride and loyalty.

Mississippi State athletics has provided me many extremely proud moments and some lasting treasured memories. Football bowl games, NCAA tournaments in basketball, College World Series baseball games, and exciting achievements in virtually every sport are the milestones of our friendship. It has been my pleasure to see Mississippi State achieve team and individual championships in the nation's best athletic conference. But it's the people who have made the moments special. Mississippi State athletics has produced some of the finest coaches and administrators in the profession. I'm proud of our association and the chance to call them all my friends.

As Mississippi State celebrates 125 years of serving the world, it remains in many ways unchanged from those days when I sat in the late Dudy Noble's office. Yet, positive progress has occurred rapidly in nearly every aspect of athletic life. It's still a great place. And you can wrap that in maroon and white!

JACK CRISTIL

Jack Cristil has served as Mississippi State's sole football play-by-play broadcaster since 1953 and has broadcast MSU basketball games since the 1957-1958 season. A member of the Army Air Corps during World War II, he studied broadcast journalism at the University of Minnesota. He received the prestigious Chris Schenkel Award in 1997 – the ABC announcer was the initial recipient in 1996 – for excellence in college broadcasting. He is a member of the Mississippi Sports Hall of Fame and a recipient of the Ronald Reagan Lifetime Achievement Award. Cristil has been named Mississippi Sportscaster of the Year a record twenty-one times and was a Southeastern Conference Broadcaster of the Year.

MSU ATHLETIC MEDIA RELATIONS

Clanging their cowbells,
students cheer from their
section of Scott Field
during a 1960s football
game that appears to be
homecoming because
the females are
wearing corsages.

Current (2003) athletic
director Larry Templeton
has taken MSU to
unparalleled heights since
taking over the Bulldog
program in 1987.

MSU administrator
and sports publicist
Bob Hartley devoted
more than fifty years
of his life to promoting
Bulldog athletics.

Cheerleaders lead the funeral procession in 1939 for Bully. The beloved bulldog was buried on the fifty-yard line of the football field. The story made *Life* magazine.

Supporting a good cause. A student's shaved head reads, "Go to Hell Ole Miss." MSU students and alumni have been known to go to extremes in showing their zeal for the Dawgs.

Playing the Fight Song, the Famous Maroon Band leads fans to Scott Field on a beautiful fall day in the 1990s.

MSU ARCHIVES

A packed stadium
watches Mississippi State
defeat Georgetown 14-7
in the 1941 Orange Bowl.

Mississippi State's Davis Wade Stadium at Scott Field, the nation's second-oldest on-campus football facility, was expanded to a capacity of 55,082 in 2001.

MSU ATHLETIC MEDIA RELATIONS

MSU ATHLETIC MEDIA RELATIONS

The Bulldogs won the 1998 SEC Western Division Championship in football, earning the school's first berth to the SEC Championship Game in Atlanta, Georgia, where they played eventual national champion, Tennessee.

Scott Field, 1923. Faculty housing is visible on one side of the field; the stands are on the other.

MSU ARCHIVES

The Mississippi State
Maroons gained national
attention in 1935 by
beating the previously
undefeated Army
team 13-7.

MSU ARCHIVES

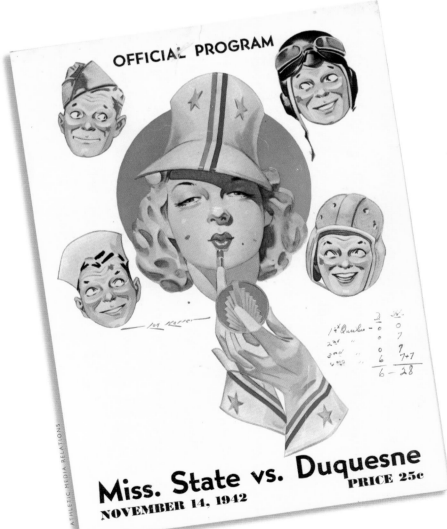

The influence of
World War II can be
seen on the cover
of the program for the
Mississippi State vs.
Duquesne homecoming
game November 14, 1942.

98

MSU ARCHIVES

Coach Allyn McKeen, *left*, accepts a plaque from CBS announcer Ted Husing during a break in practice at the 1941 Orange Bowl. McKeen is the second winningest football coach by victories.

Players on the 1941 Mississippi State team autographed the game ball after defeating Ole Miss 6-0.

PRESENTATION OF GOLDEN EGG
NOV. 21, 1936 — MISS. STATE 26 — OLE MISS. 6
Reading Left to Right
1. Major Ralph Sasse — Head Coach Miss. State   4. Paul B. Johnson Jr. — Pres. Stud. Ass. Ole Miss.
2. Bod Caldwell — Pres. Stud. Ass. Miss. State   5. Dr. G. D. Humphreys — Pres. Miss. State
3. Dr. Benny Butts — Chancelor Ole Miss.

MSU ARCHIVES

The Golden Egg trophy is awarded to Mississippi State following its 1936 defeat of Ole Miss. A&M and Ole Miss first played October 26, 1901, and the Aggies won. The first Egg Bowl was played November 25, 1927; Ole Miss won 27-12. Thanksgiving night 2003 marks the 100th meeting of the teams.

A ticket for the 1927 Egg Bowl cost $2.50.

MSU ARCHIVES

All-American D.D. Lewis later starred with the Dallas Cowboys, playing in five Super Bowls, and has been inducted into the National Football Foundation Hall of Fame.

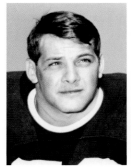

MSU ATHLETIC MEDIA RELATIONS

MSU ATHLETIC MEDIA RELATIONS

All-American quarterback Jackie Parker, who still holds MSU's single-season scoring record of 120 points, is a National Football Foundation Hall of Fame inductee.

Billy Jackson's recovery of Don Jacobs' fumble, with four seconds remaining in regulation, seals MSU's 6-3 upset win over No. 1 Alabama in 1980 at Memorial Stadium in Jackson, Mississippi. The win, which ranks among the biggest in school history, broke the Crimson Tide's twenty-eight game winning streak.

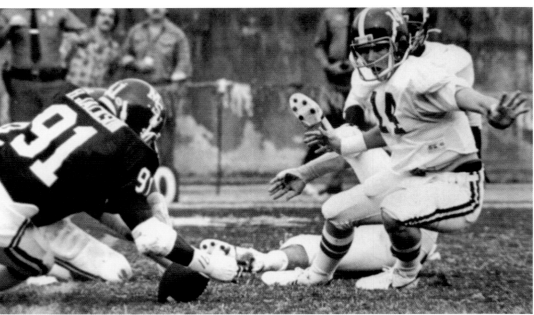

MSU ATHLETIC MEDIA RELATIONS

Mississippi State fans proudly promoted their 1998 SEC Western Division Championship team. The Bulldogs lost the SEC Championship game to Tennessee.

PAUL W. GRIMES

Kent Hull (1979–1982)
enjoyed a successful
career in the National
Football League, starring
for the Buffalo Bills
from 1986 to 1996 and
earning All-Pro honors
three times.

Current (2003) head
football coach Jackie
Sherrill has taken MSU
to half of its bowl
appearances in school
history. He also has
amassed the most wins
in school history.

Rockey Felker helped
MSU score many
victories as a player,
including this 1974 Sun
Bowl title over North
Carolina. He was named
the *Nashville Banner's*
SEC Most Valuable Player
that season and later
served as head football
coach at his alma mater,
from 1986 to 1990.

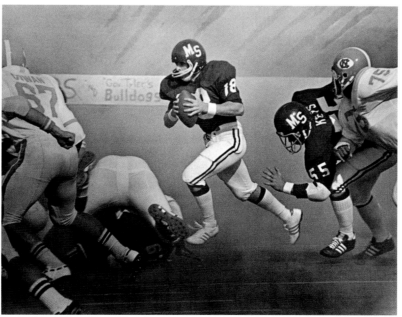

Babe McCarthy earned
SEC Coach of the Year
honors three straight
years (1961–1963), while
guiding MSU to four
SEC championships
during a five-year span
(1959–1963).

The Hump. Humphrey
Coliseum has served as
MSU's basketball home
since 1975.

The Loyola Ramblers
found enough seams in
the Bulldogs' defense to
craft a 61-51 victory in the
first round of the 1963
NCAA tournament. The
MSU team defied court

orders as it competed
against the racially
integrated Loyola
(Chicago) team in the
game played at East
Lansing, Michigan.

Jim Ashmore was an
All-American in 1956 and
1957. He stands as
Mississippi State's third
leading scorer of all time,
behind Jeff Malone and
Bailey Howell.

Hoops stars Jeff Malone,
right, and Bailey Howell
are the top two scorers in
MSU basketball history.

Coach Richard Williams,
right, head basketball
coach from 1987 to 1998,
led MSU to its first
NCAA Final Four
appearance in 1996 with
the leadership of stars
like Darryl Wilson.

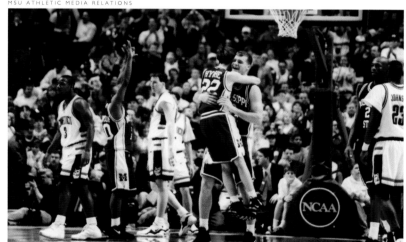

Logo for the 1996 Final
Four at the Meadowlands
in New Jersey.

Bulldogs Bart Hyche, 22,
and Russell Walters
celebrate MSU's 60-55
win over Connecticut in
the 1996 NCAA
tournament's regional

semifinals in Lexington,
Kentucky. State defeated
Cincinnati 73-63 two days
later to earn a berth in the
NCAA Final Four.

LaToya Thomas, the all-time high scorer among MSU men and women, with 2,981 career points, became just the sixth player in NCAA history to be named a four-time Kodak All-American. Thomas was selected as the No. 1 draft pick by the Cleveland Rockets in the 2003 WNBA draft.

FRED FAULK

Sharon Fanning, head women's basketball coach since 1995, is the winningest women's coach, both by percentage and by victories. She has led the women Bulldogs to their first NCAA tournament play (four overall) and the NIT twice.

MSU ATHLETIC MEDIA RELATIONS

MSU ATHLETIC MEDIA RELATIONS

A three-time All-SEC selection, Sharon Thompson was the first Lady Bulldog to be drafted into the American Basketball League. As the sixth overall pick in the 1998 draft, she was chosen by the San Jose Lasers.

A 2001 aerial view of
Dudy Noble Field/Polk-
DeMent Stadium.

RUSS HOUSTON

Mississippi A&M
College is in the field
and Louisiana State
University at bat as they
play at Hardy Athletic
Field April 12, 1907.

UNIVERSITY RELATIONS

The Left Field Lounge
area at Dudy Noble Field/
Polk-DeMent Stadium
has gained nationwide
attention as part of MSU's
baseball legend.

MSU ATHLETIC MEDIA RELATIONS

A&M was the champion baseball team of the South in 1909.

Enough to make opponents lose sleep. SEC pitchers didn't rest well the nights before they faced MSU when Rafael Palmeiro, *left*, and Will Clark were in the lineup. Together, they own several school offensive records. Both went on to successful Major League careers.

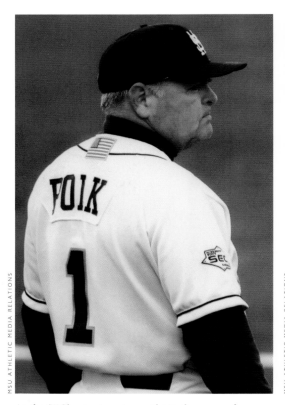

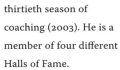

As the SEC's winningest baseball coach, MSU's Ron Polk had posted nearly 1,200 victories overall through his thirtieth season of coaching (2003). He is a member of four different Halls of Fame.

Bobby Thigpen, a star on MSU's 1985 College World Series team, set the Major League Baseball record for saves in a season in 1990. His mark still stands in 2003.

Former head baseball coach Paul Gregory directed the 1965 team to Mississippi State's first SEC championship, its first of four titles under his tutelage.

Former Diamond Dog Nat "Buck" Showalter, *left,* manager for the Texas Rangers in 2003, was inducted into the MSU Sports Hall of Fame in fall 2002. Showalter sits next to Major League Baseball Hall of Famer Mickey Mantle during Showalter's time as the New York Yankee skipper (1992–1995).

C.R. "Dudy" Noble coached baseball from 1920 to 1947 and football in 1922. He was the school's athletic director from 1930 to 1934. MSU's baseball field is named for him.

Boo Ferriss lettered at MSU (1941–1942) and went on to an outstanding pro baseball career with the Boston Red Sox. He was inducted into the Red Sox Hall of Fame in 2002.

The 1923 track team included C.S. Cochran, *fourth from right*, who won a gold medal in the 1924 Olympics as he helped set a world record time for the 4 × 100. *Second from right*, W.O. Spencer, for whom the track field and stadium are named, also won a gold medal and helped set a world record in the 4 × 100.

1923

MSU ARCHIVES

Garry Frank, MSU's record holder in the shot put and discus, won the 1987 NCAA outdoor shot put title.

MSU ATHLETIC MEDIA RELATIONS

MSU ATHLETIC MEDIA RELATIONS

Festus Igbinoghene (1988–1991) was a six-time track All-American.

Nigerian Falilath Ogunkoya was a five-time All-American as a member of the Lady Bulldogs track team. She won silver and bronze medals for the 4 × 100 and 400-meter events, respectively, as she represented her native country in the 1996 Olympics.

MSU ATHLETIC MEDIA RELATIONS

Arguably the most successful sprinter in school history, Lorenzo Daniel still holds the NCAA meet and MSU school records in the 200-meter dash outdoors with his 19.87 time run in 1988.

MSU ATHLETIC MEDIA RELATIONS

MSU ATHLETIC MEDIA RELATIONS

As a sophomore, Tiffany McWilliams became the most decorated female trackster in school history, winning one national and three SEC titles. Her time of 4:06.75 in the outdoor 1500-meter run set a new NCAA meet record in 2003.

Three-time All-American Marco Baron (1998–2001) was likely the most decorated MSU player ever. Ranked No. 1 in singles at the end of his senior season, he received the prestigious Arthur Ashe Sportsmanship and Leadership Award that season, as well.

MSU ATHLETIC MEDIA RELATIONS

Legendary head men's tennis coach Tom Sawyer compiled an incredible 216-36 record during his MSU coaching career from 1949 to 1968. His Bulldog teams won two Southeastern Conference championships, tied for third nationally twice, and finished among the country's top fifteen four times.

MSU ATHLETIC MEDIA RELATIONS

MSU ATHLETIC MEDIA RELATIONS

Bobby Brien was a two-time NCAA quarterfinalist in both singles (1966 and 1967) and doubles (1965 and 1967).

MSU ATHLETIC MEDIA RELATIONS

MSU's Claire Pollard, *left*, and Jackie Holden celebrate winning the 1989 NCAA women's doubles championship in Gainesville, Florida.

MSU ATHLETIC MEDIA RELATIONS

Bulldog tennis standouts Laurent Miquelard, *left*, and Joc Simmons claimed the 1994 NCAA doubles championship in South Bend, Indiana.

MSU ATHLETIC MEDIA RELATIONS

Tennis coach Andy Jackson stands first on MSU's all-time coaching list for victories, with 220 from 1989 to 2001.

He led MSU to eleven straight NCAA appearances, ten of them resulting in round of sixteen or better showings.

RUSS HOUSTON

A top-down view
of volleyball action in
the 1990s.

MISSISSIPPI STATE UNIVERSITY
Volleyball/Women's Basketball
1996-97
179
Season Ticket
_____
Two (2) Admissions for $30.00
Events included in ticket plan listed on back

PAUL W. GRIMES

A pass to attend
women's basketball and
volleyball games.

Volleyball's Aimee York was named the SEC's Female Scholar-Athlete of the Year in 1992. MSU has had the second-most SEC Scholar-Athletes overall since the award's inception.

Kellie Wilkerson was a four-time (1999–2002) NFCA All-America selection.

Mississippi State revived its softball program in 1997. Its second year, the team made the finals of the SEC tournament.

The 2001 Lady Bulldog
soccer team claimed
the SEC's Western
Division crown.

Women's soccer has been
offered at MSU since 1995.

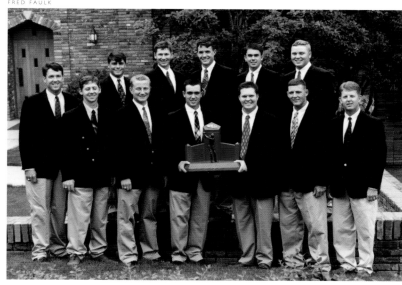

Christi Sanders has twice been named SEC Coach of the Year during her years as MSU's women's golf coach.

They know their greens. The 1997 MSU men's golf team won the SEC Championship. Team members pose with their trophy in front of the Chapel of Memories.

The women's golf program had included one SEC individual champion (1992) and six All-Americans as of 2003.

This field, *above*, produced potatoes in 1899. The next crop, twenty years later, was turpentine from trees.

A biochemistry and molecular biology professor examines plants in tubes, *left*.

Mississippi State University today enjoys the status of a national research university, ranking fifty-seventh among all United States public institutions of higher learning in research expenditures, as reported by the National Science Foundation for 2001. With research activity exceeding $147 million that year, MSU was third among Southeastern Conference schools, fifth among all institutions in agriculture, and its James W. Bagley College of Engineering was thirty-second of 330 engineering schools.

Today's research and outreach are far different from that of the first seventy-five years. About the only research conducted then was in agricultural sciences and forestry, funded by a separate state appropriation and federal monies from the Cooperative State Research Service of the U.S. Department of Agriculture. Likewise, outreach consisted only of Mississippi Cooperative Extension Service programs, funded jointly by the state and federal governments. With an office, agents, and home demonstration personnel in every county, the Extension Service was Mississippi's primary conduit for the transfer of agricultural research results and services to farmers, their families, and developing agricultural industries.

Dr. August Raspet, a distinguished engineer and scientist, came to Mississippi State in 1949 to establish an aerophysics research program. It became the first non-agricultural research to attract federal funding, starting with a $32,000 Office of Naval Research grant. The next year saw the development of a Social Science Research Center, resulting from a visionary combination of a Social Science Roundtable with the Rural Sociology Department in agriculture.

A landmark administrative reorganization in 1961 set the stage for other university units to take advantage of new federal support for graduate studies and research. Four vice presidents were named, and an Office of Research and Graduate Studies was established. ORGS was headed by a dean of the graduate school and coordinator of research, a title that changed in 1969 to vice president.

Successes followed in competitions for graduate fellowships, individual faculty research contracts, teaching and research equipment grants, and facilities grants. By its centennial, Mississippi State had the fully developed roots to support exponential growth in doctoral programs and research.

The images that follow highlight MSU's long-term contributions to new knowledge from research and its services to people through diverse and effective outreach programs.

As the son of a botany professor, Chester McKee grew up at Mississippi State from infancy through his enrollment as a freshman in 1941. He joined the Navy midway through college but completed his electrical engineering degree in 1944. He attended the University of Wisconsin-Madison, receiving his master of science in 1949 and his doctorate in 1952.

After teaching at Mississippi State for a number of years, he became head of the Electrical Engineering Department in 1957. He was named dean of the Graduate School and coordinator of research in 1962. He retired in 1979 as professor emeritus of electrical engineering and vice president emeritus for research and graduate studies.

He served as a director at the National Research Council from 1979 to 1989.

CHESTER MCKEE

Workers fill a silo in
the 1930s. A campus
building is visible in
the background.

A 1941 photo compares
a plot fertilized with
phosphate and potash,
left, with a plot fertilized
with phosphate only.
The experiment was
part of a Mississippi
Experiment Station
program.

The Animal Research
Center of the Mississippi
Agricultural and Forestry
Experiment Station is
located on the main
campus. Researchers in
aquaculture, beef cattle,
poultry, sheep, and other
areas use these facilities
for their various projects.

Responding to the call to grow other crops besides cotton, Corn Clubs appeared throughout Mississippi at the turn of the twentieth century. W.H. "Corn Club" Smith, *second from right*, organized the first such club in Holmes County in 1907. From the Corn Clubs grew the 4-H movement that would spread nationwide. Smith became the state's first supervisor of rural education in 1910, the same year this photo was taken. In 1916, he became the fifth president of Mississippi A&M College. *Standing in the center of the group* is W.B. Lundy, the first Mississippi State county agent.

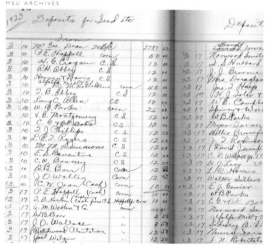

A daybook from the Delta Experiment Station shows entries in the livestock and soybean accounts, offering insights into farm finances in 1923.

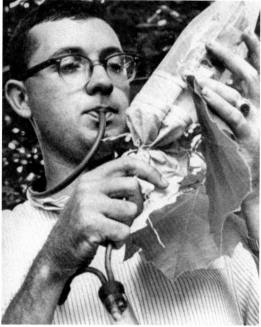

It's all in a day's work for an entomologist, featured in a 1970 *Reveille* photo as he uses an aspirator to take leafhoppers from a rearing cage.

The campus dairy has produced milk since the days of one-pint glass bottles.

SARA E. MORRIS

"Builds strong Bulldogs" might be the slogan of MSU milk, a strong seller in 2003.

PAUL W. GRIMES

MSU EXTENTION SERVICE

A MAFES agronomist checks data from the global positioning system mounted on his four-wheeler in 1998. The GPS system uses data it receives from eight satellites to draw field maps with precise soil-sampling locations.

FRED FAULK

A picturesque fall day in the 1980s finds a student and three others watching as cotton is picked.

The Meats Laboratory is located on Stone Boulevard, across from Dorman Hall. Operated for teaching and research in meats, the lab serves the Animal and Dairy Sciences Department and the Food Science and Technology Department. Its products, including ground beef, pork chops, bacon, sausage, cutlets, and spareribs, generally are available for retail sale to the public.

Food science and technology employees prepare cheese for molds in the 1990s.

Say cheese. Edam, cheddar, and jalapeno pepper cheeses are among the 104,000 dairy units the Food Science and Technology Department sells annually. Milk comes from cows raised at the MAFES branches.

It's not just a cow
college anymore.
Workers harvest shrimp
in the 1980s.

First there were catfish,
then came crayfish.
A wildlife and fisheries
professor extracts
"mudbugs" in the rice pond.

Enologists evaluate
muscadines used in wine
research in the 1970s.
These days the grapes are
used to make grape juice,
ice cream, and other
products.

Mississippi Agricultural and Forestry
Experiment Station

Muscadine
Grape
Juice

School of Human Sciences
Mississippi State, MS 39762
Ingredients: Muscadine Juice, Citric Acid, Potassium Sorbate

Online muscadine?
The School of Human
Sciences and Mississippi
Agricultural and Forestry
Experiment Station
cooperate to manufacture
muscadine grape juice,
available on the
MSU Web site in 2003.

Top flight. From the early to mid 1990s, aircraft in the Raspet Flight Research Lab (RFRL) included a Marvel II, Rockwell Turbo Commander 690, NASP X-30, and Stearman PT-17. One of the finest university flight research facilities in the nation, RFRL is named for Mississippi State College professor August Raspet, who founded the lab in 1948.

JIM HENSON

MSU ARCHIVES

Dr. George Bennett, *left*, tests the feasibility of an ornithopter, an aircraft propelled by flapping wings, in 1980. Bennett, an aerospace engineering professor, also was head of the Raspet Flight Research Lab.

MSU ARCHIVES

Aerospace engineering experiments with plane design in the 1960s.

FRED FAULK

Framed by the stable door, a horse is led by workers on a typical day at the farm.

FRED FAULK

Students, faculty, and staff conduct several tests on horses on the South Farm.

The tools of terracing have changed through the years. A Martin ditcher and horses get the job done in the 1930s.

MSU ARCHIVES

FRED FAULK

A worker demonstrates a procedure to three others – and the photographer, whose shadow is visible – on the South Farm in the 1980s.

A Forest Products Laboratory technician displays a composition board made of shredded waste paper sprayed with a pulp wood by-product in the 1980s. The lab houses the analytical and testing equipment, pilot plants, and support facilities required for comprehensive research of wood and wood products.

Dissertation research. A doctoral candidate in physical chemistry uses a fluorescence microscope to study protein crystals.

Science in the 1960s. A professor conducts an experiment in a Dorman Hall laboratory.

Two professors and an installer look over the first analog computer on campus, taking up almost an entire room in 1965.

A student inputs data into a UNIVAC computer in 1978. Because he is in the "express line," he must limit his input to six cards when others are waiting.

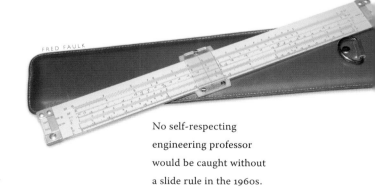

No self-respecting engineering professor would be caught without a slide rule in the 1960s.

The Diagnostic Instrumentation and Analysis Laboratory, established in 1980, is an interdisciplinary research department in the College of Engineering. The lab employs modern diagnostic techniques to monitor, control, and optimize processes to improve process understanding while minimizing environmental impact.

FRED FAULK

The Mississippi Research and Technology Park, adjacent to MSU, is on land once used as a university dairy farm. The park is home to three major university research centers: the Diagnostic Instrumentation and Analysis Laboratory, the Engineering Research Center, and the Social Science Research Center.

FRED FAULK

ENGINEERING RESEARCH CENTER

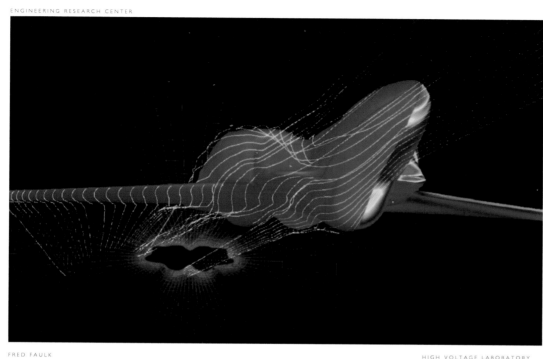

A 2000 computer graphic inside the Engineering Research Center.

FRED FAULK

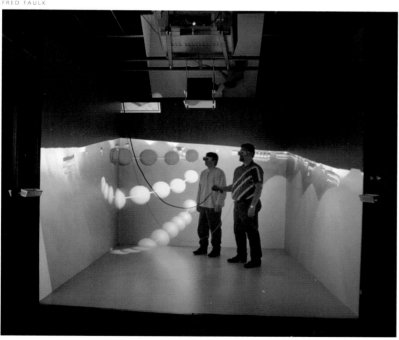

The Cove is a virtual room-sized environment at the Engineering Research Center.

HIGH VOLTAGE LABORATORY

A lightning stroke terminates at the lightning rod of a model naval warship in 2000. The High Voltage Lab runs research projects on lightning protection for different systems, such as warships and aircraft.

Experimentation, 2003.
Graduate students conduct
a test at the Diagnostic
Instrumentation and
Analysis Laboratory.

FRED FAULK

A professor instructs a
student at a 1960 business
seminar. Behind them,
a graph shows Mississippi's
business activity index
increasing over the past
few years.

MSU ARCHIVES

Students and local townspeople view a tank demonstration in 1917, during World War I.

May Quarles, *in the dark dress,* attends a short course with agents who were part of the Extension Service in 1918.

FRED FAULK

One-of-a kind center. An employee of the Rehabilitation Research and Training Center on Blindness and Low Vision uses a closed-circuit television and magnification software to enlarge printed material. The center is the only one of its type in the nation. Its training projects focus on employment and career development for individuals who are blind or have low vision.

Pet project. College of Veterinary Medicine student volunteers introduce their furry friends to residents of a local retirement center.

TOM THOMPSON

The Cobb Institute
of Archaeology
Virtual Museum
Collection includes the
ceramic horned bull,
Babylonian rhyton,
Ca. 2,500–1,500 B.C.

COBB INSTITUTE OF ARCHAEOLOGY VIRTUAL MUSEUM

DUANE GILL

Earthwatch volunteers assist an MSU social science researcher in studying the social disruption and psychological stress of the *Exxon Valdez* oil spill on private property in Alaska. The National Science Foundation provided the grant, which began in 1989.

The *Mississippi Statistical Abstract* is published annually by MSU's Office of Business Research and Services, College of Business and Industry.

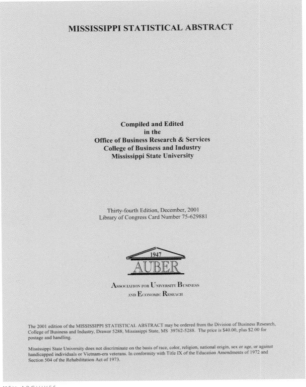

MISSISSIPPI STATISTICAL ABSTRACT

Compiled and Edited
in the
Office of Business Research & Services
College of Business and Industry
Mississippi State University

Thirty-fourth Edition, December, 2001
Library of Congress Card Number 75-629881

1947
AUBER
ASSOCIATION FOR UNIVERSITY BUSINESS
AND ECONOMIC RESEARCH

The 2001 edition of the MISSISSIPPI STATISTICAL ABSTRACT may be ordered from the Division of Business Research, College of Business and Industry, Drawer 5288, Mississippi State, MS 39762-5288. The price is $40.00, plus $2.00 for postage and handling.

Mississippi State University does not discriminate on the basis of race, color, religion, national origin, sex or age, or against handicapped individuals or Vietnam-era veterans. In conformity with Title IX of the Education Amendments of 1972 and Section 504 of the Rehabilitation Act of 1973.

MSU ARCHIVES

MSU ARCHIVES

Members of a Mississippi Home Demonstration Club learn how to refinish furniture in the 1930s. Extension programs helped Mississippians learn inexpensive, practical ways to improve their standard of living.

Perhaps no one appreciates the beauty of the land-grant university more than the operator of this cotton picker, nearing sundown in the 1980s.

FRED FAULK

Mississippi Quarterly, The Journal of Southern Cultures, has been published since 1948.

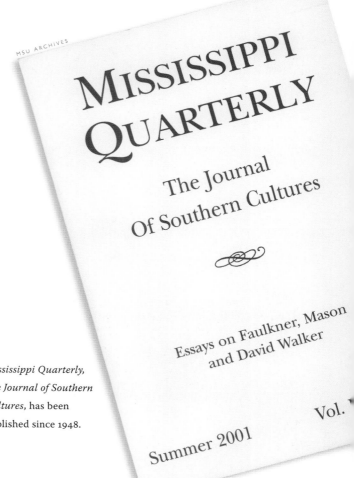

MSU ARCHIVES

MISSISSIPPI QUARTERLY

The Journal Of Southern Cultures

Essays on Faulkner, Mason and David Walker

Summer 2001   Vol.

Research begins in the library. As the saying goes, "An hour in the library will save you many hours in the lab."

Two economics professors in the College of Business and Industry work on an econometrics problem as part of their research.

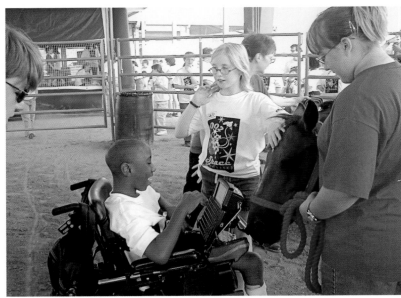

Camp Jabber Jaw provides a fun way for individuals to develop improved interactive communication skills. Each year approximately forty to fifty campers, staff members, family, and friends from Mississippi, Alabama, Louisiana, and Texas participate in the week-long activities. A camper has fun with a horse as he and others enjoy a day at the Horse Park, 2002.

The view from above.
A satellite image of
North Farm.

MSU REMOTE SENSING TECHNOLOGIES CENTER

An aerial view of the
Delta Research and
Extension Center in
Stoneville, Mississippi.
The center is one of the
largest agricultural
experiment stations in the
world, situated on some
of the best agricultural
lands in the Yazoo
Mississippi Delta.

MSU OFFICE OF AGRICULTURAL COMMUNICATIONS

137

MAROON AND WHITE
Alma Mater

In the heart of Mississippi
Made by none but God's own hands
Stately in her nat'ral splendor
Our Alma Mater proudly stands.
State College of Mississippi,
Fondest mem'ries cling to thee,
Life shall hoard thy spirit ever,
Loyal sons we'll always be.

Chorus:
Maroon and White! Maroon and White!
Of thee with joy we sing.
Thy colors bright, our souls delight,
With praise our voices ring.

Tho' our life some pow'r vanquish,
Loyalty can't be o'er run;
Honors true on thee we lavish
Until the setting of the sun;
Live Maroon and White for ever,
Ne'er can evil mar thy fame,
Nothing us from thee can sever,
Alma Mater we acclaim.

ACKNOWLEDGEMENTS

SPECIAL THANKS ARE EXTENDED
TO THE FOLLOWING:

Richard Armstrong, executive director, MSU Foundation

Dr. Mike Ballard, coordinator, Congressional Collections, MSU Libraries

Nancy Bardwell, student

Connie Black, administrative secretary, Aerospace Engineering

Raymond Brooks, associate director, Colvard Union

Janie Cirlot-New, M.S., CCC/SLP, director, T.K. Martin Center for Technology and Disability

John Cruickshank, librarian, Veterinary Medicine Library

Dr. Lou D'Abramo, professor, Wildlife and Fisheries

Dr. Duane Gill, research professor, Social Science Research Center

Dr. Paul W. Grimes, professor and Department Head, Finance and Economics

Dr. Stanley Grzybowski, professor, Electrical and Computer Engineering

Alexa Harris, student

Cindy Harris, library assistant, MSU Libraries

Russell Houston, photographer, University Relations

Paul Huddleston, systems and networks manager, MSU Libraries

Jim Lytle, chief photographer, Office of Agricultural Communications

Beth Morgan, student worker, University Relations

Dr. J. Elton Moore, director, RRTC on Blindness and Low Vision

The MSU Athletic Media Relations Office

Dr. Craig Piper, archivist, Congressional and Political Research Center and University Archives

Dr. Roy Poole, professor, CVM Pathobiology

Dr. David Shaw, professor, director, Remote Sensing Technology Center

Staff, Special Collections, MSU Libraries

Lyle Tate, library assistant, MSU Libraries

Melanie Thomas, librarian, MSU Meridian Branch Library

Tom Thompson, medical photographer, Agricultural Communications

Rob Thornton, computer services assistant, MSU Libraries

Timothy Vann, MSU Bookstore Manager

Anita Winger, computer services assistant, MSU Libraries

Members of the 125th Anniversary Steering Committee:

Emma Armstrong, facilities scheduling administrator, Support Services

Dr. Ann Bailey, director, Housing and Residence Life

Kristy Brown, Starkville Chamber of Commerce

John Cade, assistant director, Media Relations, Athletic Department

Dr. Walter Diehl, professor, Biological Sciences

Joe Farris, director, University Relations/President's Office

Dr. Mike Fazio, interim associate dean, Architecture

Dr. Rodney Foil, emeritus vice president, Agriculture, Forestry, and Veterinary Medicine

Maridith Geuder, associate director, University Relations

Marybeth Grimes, reference librarian, MSU Libraries

Dr. Sandra Harpole, interim associate vice president, Research

Marilyn James, coordinator, Financial Aid, Records, and Registration, Meridian Campus

Blane Merritt, Division of External Affairs

Dennis Prescott, committee chair, vice president, External Affairs

Dr. Lynn Reinschmiedt, associate dean, College of Agriculture and Life Sciences

Michael Richardson, coordinator, Chapter Program, Alumni Activities

Stacy Roberson, director, Holmes Cultural Diversity Center

Dr. Roy Ruby, dean, College of Education

Brenda Thornton, class of 1978, executive vice president/CIO, AmFed Co. LLC

Charles Weatherly, (Ret.) senior director, Development, MSU Foundation

Dale Welch, graduate studies manager, Office of Graduate Studies

Parker Wiseman, student, president, Student Association

125th Anniversary Book Subcommittee:

Dr. Ann Bailey, director, Housing and Residence Life

Fred Faulk, coordinator, Photographic Services, University Relations

Cris L. Ferguson, serials librarian, MSU Libraries

Maridith Geuder, associate director, University Relations

Marybeth Grimes, committee chair, reference librarian, MSU Libraries

Sara E. Morris, reference librarian, MSU Libraries

Michael Richardson, coordinator, Chapter Program, Alumni Activities

Betty Self, library associate, MSU Libraries

Elizabeth Urbanik, serials cataloger, MSU Libraries

This book was designed by Addison Hall,
art directed by Hilda Stauss Owen,
and edited by Brenda Trigg
of Communication Arts Company in Jackson, Mississippi.
It was printed by Hederman Brothers in Ridgeland, Mississippi,
in a first edition of 10,000 copies.

The typeface is Warnock Pro,
designed by Robert Slimbach,
issued in digital form by Adobe Systems,
Mountain View, California.

The paper is Sheufelen PhoenoStar,
an acid and chlorine-free art paper.